SCOTTISH SONGS FOR GUITAR

How to play 15 Scottish classics, with standard notation and tablature, complete lyrics, and background information

By Danny Carnahan

string letter media

Publisher: David A. Lusterman
Editor: Adam Perlmutter
Managing Editor: Kevin Owens
Design and Production: Bill Evans
Production Manager: Hugh O'Connor

Cover Photograph: Joey Lusterman

ISBN 978-0-9626081-4-8

Printed in the United States of America
This book was produced by Stringletter Media, Inc.
501 Canal Blvd., Suite J, Richmond, CA 94804
(510) 215-0010; stringletter.com

Contents

Introduction 4

A Word About Scots Lyrics 5

Notation Guide 6

SONGS IN STANDARD TUNING

The Rigs of Barley 10

Both Sides the Tweed 13

Rattlin' Roarin' Willie 17

Will Ye Go to Flanders 19

Tae the Weavers Gin Ye Gang 22

SONGS IN DROPPED-D TUNING

Cam Ye O'er Frae France 24

Hughie the Grahame 26

Glenlogie 29

Tae the Beggin' 33

So Will We Yet 36

The Wild Mountain Thyme 41

Now Westlin Winds 44

Fortune Turns the Wheel 47

The False Lover Won Back 49

Fair Flower of Northumberland 54

About the Author 58

Source Materials 59

Video downloads to accompany each of the lessons and musical examples in *Scottish Songs for Guitar* are available for free at **store.acousticguitar.com/SSFGvideo**. Just add the video tracks to your shopping cart and check out to get your free download.

Introduction

In 1983, when I stepped off a train in Edinburgh, Scotland, with the rest of my traveling California theatre troupe, I had already been a lover of Celtic traditional music for 15 years, having first been made aware of Celtic music as its own distinct genre while visiting relatives in Wales in 1968 and hearing Irish songs played on pirate radio. Several trips to Ireland since then had turned me into a rabid habitué of the pub *seisúns* (Irish music jam sessions) on both sides of the Atlantic, and I had somehow managed to make a living for the previous half a dozen years performing on the American folk club and festival circuit.

I was in Edinburgh to perform for a month at the Edinburgh Fringe Festival in a production of the Spoon River Anthology, my role being the old time musicians "Fiddler Jones." But my heart's secret desire was to spend as much time as possible in the Scots folk clubs, soaking up beer and Scottish repertoire in equal measure.

That warm, magical month changed my life. When our play finished in the evening we whipped off our costumes and our most obvious makeup, sprinting across the street to the nearest pub with music happening. We'd play till closing time; we'd follow the tipsy crowd to another pub with an extended license and play till they kicked us out. Then we'd wander down to the Turkish kebab joint that was open till four in the morning. There was nowhere to go from four till five, when the local bakery started selling buns out the back door, so we'd all sit in the park and keep playing. I remember Gerald Trimble playing cittern in a tree, and I don't remember sleeping much.

But oh, the music—and the musicians. What a glorious stroke of luck to be in Edinburgh just when that creativity grenade went off. The first seisún I joined was led by Jim Sutherland, whose driving cittern playing was otherworldly in its power. Johnnie and Phil Cunningham blew through town, as did Dick Gaughan and Brian McNeill. Within days I blissed out at the farewell concert by Jock Tamson's Bairns—a pivotal moment in Scots trad history as guitarist Rod Paterson joined up with Jim Sutherland to form The Easy Club and fellow guitarist Tony Cuffe joined forces with Ossian. While Ossian took the tradition into a highly textured dreamworld, The Easy Club injected a swing and fire that it still hasn't lost.

And then there were the singers: Dougie MacLean, Mary Macmaster, and Patsy Seddon, among many others. All cheek by jowl, jumbled together in cramped little rooms, making such glorious music I thought my heart would explode. And they all treated us California interlopers as long-lost kin. They took us home and fed us dinner. They sat for hours teaching us songs and playing tunes and songs into our bottomless tape recorders. Dougie and his wife passed their baby around the pint-strewn pub table to the delight of all. A changed life, indeed.

So, 30-odd years on I find myself putting together a set of Scottish songs, most of which I have performed over the decades, and each of which takes me back to that magical Edinburgh summer. I can never thank all my old Edinburgh friends—both denizens and fellow wanderers of the tour circuit—enough for setting me off so solidly on this path. I can only encourage you to hunt up as many recordings as you can and go back to the sources like those that first inspired me. There's a list of recordings and other sources at the end of this book to get you started. And while Johnnie Cunningham and Tony Cuffe and a few others have joined the cosmic *ceilidh*, many of these great musicians are still touring. So go hear them live. And then go home, grab your guitar, and take the tradition wherever it wants to go. —*Danny Carnahan*

A Word About Scots Lyrics

I am persuaded that Scottish (or Scots) is less a dialect of English than its own distinct language. There are large overlaps in syntax and vocabulary with standard English, but where the two do not overlap, Scots can start sounding pretty darn alien. And since I am not Scottish-born, I don't wish to pass myself off as a native singer in Scots.

I admit that in the days of my most youthful Celtic zeal, I tried to sing exactly the way I heard the songs on records. But a phony accent seemed to do the songs a disservice. These songs, after all, contain powerful emotional truths, tremendous narratives, great humor, and simply wonderful poetry. I'd rather let the song do its work, and—as much as possible—get out of its way.

The settings of the song lyrics I've included in this collection are versions intended for the wider English-speaking audience. Some of the Scottish words or phrases have been altered, with as light a touch as possible, the goal being to sacrifice none of the lilt and lightness of the Scottish phrasing.

Some straightforward switch-outs were possible in service of storytelling clarity. In the concluding verse of "Glenlogie," for instance, I substituted "her dowry's been told" for the Scots "her tocher's doun tauld." And the common use of "wi'" for "with" comes and goes in this collection, depending, I think, on my original source for each song. I anglicized to "with" in "The Rigs of Barley" but left it shortened in "Rattlin' Roarin' Willie." Go figure.

"Tae the Weavers" is presented here in quite broad Scots, because it's fun to sing that way, even though some of the lines require a bit of a context stretch to work out their meanings.

The last couplet in "Tae the Weavers," noting the result of the roll in the hay, goes like this:

But what was said, or what was done, shame fa' me gin I tell
But, oh! I fear the kintra soon will ken as weel's mysel'

In more standard and far less poetic English, it means: "But what was said, or what was done, it would embarrass the heck out of me to admit, but I'm afraid the whole country will know soon what I know myself." That doesn't scan nearly as prettily, hence my retaining the Scots here.

Another lovely feature of Scots is its ability to indulge in rhymes that resist massaging into standard English. "Aw" rhymes with "awa," but if you try to standardize them to "all" and "away," there goes your rhyme. "Braw" rhymes with "blaw" but substituting "handsome" and "blow" won't do at all. As to when it's a good thing to choose Scots over standard English or the other way round in arranging a traditional song, I claim neither consistency nor scientific method.

So if you find you prefer to sing the original Scots, I say, "Bravo to that!" But I hope these versions will convey my love for the songs and for the tradition they grew out of. These are traditional songs, after all. They are living things, and each new singer adds a little something to the songs and the tradition. If you find you're changing a song a little to make it your own, you're doing something right. Experiment, explore, and may you enjoy these songs as much as I do.

Notation Guide

Reading music is no different than reading a book. In both cases, you need to understand the language that you're reading; you can't read Chinese characters if you don't understand them, and you can't read music if you don't understand the written symbols behind music notation.

Guitarists use several types of notation, including standard notation, tablature, and chord grids. Standard notation is the main notation system common to all instruments and styles in Western music. Knowing standard notation will allow you to share and play music with almost any other instrument. Tablature is a notation system exclusively for stringed instruments with frets—like guitar and mandolin—that shows you what strings and frets to play at any given moment. Chord grids use a graphic representation of the fretboard to show chord shapes for fretted stringed instruments. Here's a primer on how to read these types of notation.

Standard Notation

Standard notation is written on a five-line staff. Notes are written in alphabetical order from A to G. Every time you pass a G note, the sequence of notes repeats—starting with A.

The duration of a note is determined by three things: the note head, stem, and flag. A whole note (o) equals four beats. A half note (d) is half of that: two beats. A quarter note (♩) equals one beat, an eighth note (♪) equals half of one beat, and a 16th note (♬) is a quarter beat (there are four 16th notes per beat).

The fraction (4/4, 3/4, 6/8, etc.) or c character shown at the beginning of a piece of music denotes the time signature. The top number tells you how many beats are in each measure, and the bottom number indicates the rhythmic value of each beat (4 equals a quarter note, 8 equals an eighth note, 16 equals a 16th note, and 2 equals a half note).

The most common time signature is 4/4, which signifies four quarter notes per measure and is sometimes designated with the symbol c (for common time). The symbol ¢ stands for cut time (2/2). Most songs are either in 4/4 or 3/4.

Tablature

In tablature, the six horizontal lines represent the six strings of the guitar, with the first string on the top and sixth on the bottom. The numbers refer to fret numbers on a given string.

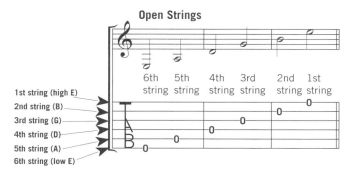

The notation and tablature in this book are designed to be used in tandem—refer to the notation to get the rhythmic information and note durations, and refer to the tablature to get the exact locations of the notes on the guitar fingerboard.

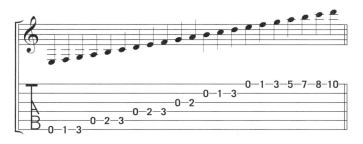

Fingerings

Fingerings are indicated with small numbers and letters in the notation. Fretting-hand fingering is indicated with 1 for the index finger, 2 the middle, 3 the ring, 4 the pinky, and *T* the thumb. Picking-hand fingering is indicated by *i* for the index finger, *m* the middle, *a* the ring, *c* the pinky, and *p* the thumb. Circled numbers indicate the string the note is played on. Remember that the fingerings indicated are only suggestions; if you find a different way that works better for you, use it.

Strumming and Picking

In music played with a flatpick, downstrokes (toward the floor) and upstrokes (toward the ceiling) are shown as follows. Slashes in the notation and tablature indicate a strum through the previously played chord.

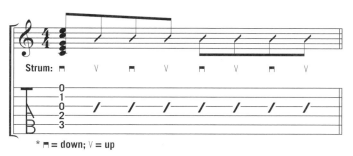

* ⊓ = down; V = up

In music played with the pick-hand fingers, *split stems* are often used to highlight the division between thumb and fingers. With split stems, notes played by the thumb have stems pointing down, while notes played by the fingers have stems pointing up. If split stems are not used, pick-hand fingerings are usually present. Here is the same fingerpicking pattern shown with and without split stems.

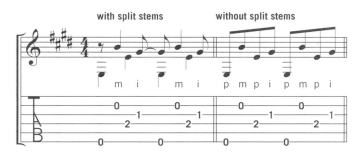

Chord Diagrams

Chord diagrams show where the fingers go on the fingerboard. Frets are shown horizontally. The thick top line represents the nut. A fret number to the right of a diagram indicates a chord played higher up the neck (in this case the top horizontal line is thin). Strings are shown as vertical lines. The line on the far left represents the sixth (lowest) string, and the line on the far right represents the first (highest) string. Dots show where the fingers go, and thick horizontal lines indicate barres. Numbers above the diagram are left-hand finger numbers, as used in standard notation.

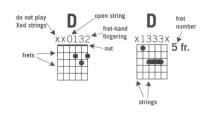

Again, the fingerings are only suggestions. An *X* indicates a string that should be muted or not played; 0 indicates an open string.

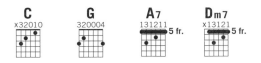

Capos

If a capo is used, a Roman numeral indicates the fret where the capo should be placed. The standard notation and tablature is written as if the capo were the nut of the guitar. For instance, a tune capoed anywhere up the neck and played using key-of-G chord shapes and fingerings will be written in the key of G. Likewise, open strings held down by the capo are written as open strings.

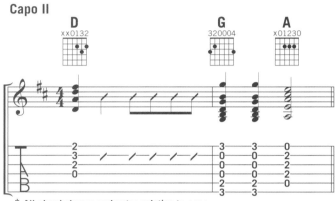

*All chord shapes and notes relative to capo

Tunings

Alternate guitar tunings are given from the lowest (sixth) string to the highest (first) string. For instance, D A D G B E indicates standard tuning with the bottom string dropped to D. Standard notation for songs in alternate tunings always reflects the actual pitches of the notes. Arrows underneath tuning notes indicate strings that are altered from standard tuning and whether they are tuned up or down.

Tuning: D A D G B E

Vocal Tunes

Vocal tunes are sometimes written with a fully tabbed-out introduction and a vocal melody with chord diagrams for the rest of the piece. The tab intro is usually your indication of which strum or fingerpicking pattern to use in the rest of the piece. The melody with lyrics underneath is the melody sung by the vocalist. Occasionally, smaller notes are written with the melody to indicate other instruments or the harmony part sung by another vocalist. These are not to be confused with cue notes, which are small notes that indicate melodies that vary when a section is repeated. Listen to a recording of the piece to get a feel for the guitar accompaniment and to hear the singing if you aren't skilled at reading vocal melodies.

Articulations

There are a number of ways you can articulate a note on the guitar. Notes connected with slurs (not to be confused with ties) in the tablature or standard notation are articulated with either a hammer-on, pull-off, or slide. Lower notes slurred to higher notes are played as hammer-ons; higher notes slurred to lower notes are played as pull-offs.

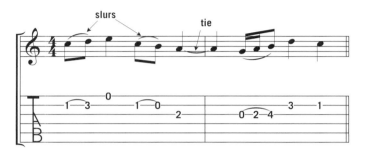

Slides are represented with a dash, and an S is included above the tab. A dash preceding a note represents a slide into the note from an indefinite point in the direction of the slide; a dash following a note indicates a slide off of the note to an indefinite point in the direction of the slide. For two slurred notes connected with a slide, you should pick the first note and then slide into the second.

Bends are represented with upward curves, as shown in the next example. Most bends have a specific destination pitch—the number above the bend symbol shows how much the bend raises the string's pitch: ¼ for a slight bend, ½ for a half step, 1 for a whole step.

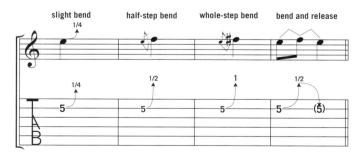

Grace notes are represented by small notes with a dash through the stem in standard notation and with small numbers in the tab. A grace note is a very quick ornament leading into a note, most commonly executed as a hammer-on, pull-off, or slide. In the first example below, pluck the note at the fifth fret on the beat, then quickly hammer onto the seventh fret. The second example is executed as a quick pull-off from the second fret to the open string. In the third example, both notes at the fifth fret are played simultaneously (even though it appears that the fifth fret, fourth string, is to be played by itself), then the seventh fret, fourth string, is quickly hammered.

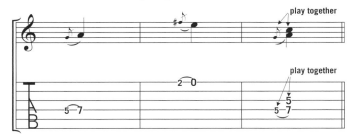

Harmonics

Harmonics are represented by diamond-shaped notes in the standard notation and a small dot next to the tablature numbers. Natural harmonics are indicated with the text "Harmonics" or "Harm." above the tablature. Harmonics articulated with the right hand (often called artificial harmonics) include the text "R.H. Harmonics" or "R.H. Harm." above the tab. Right-hand harmonics are executed by lightly touching the harmonic node (usually 12 frets above the open string or fretted note) with the right-hand index finger and plucking the string with the thumb or ring finger or pick. For extended phrases played with right-hand harmonics, the fretted notes are shown in the tab along with instructions to touch the harmonics 12 frets above the notes.

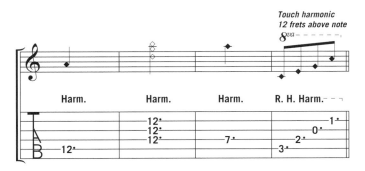

Repeats

One of the most confusing parts of a musical score can be the navigation symbols, such as repeats, *D.S. al Coda*, *D.C. al Fine*, *To Coda*, etc. Repeat symbols are placed at the beginning and end of the passage to be repeated.

You should ignore repeat symbols with the dots on the right side the first time you encounter them; when you come to a repeat symbol with dots on the left side, jump back to the previous repeat symbol facing the opposite direction (if there is no previous symbol, go to the beginning of the piece). The next time you come to the repeat symbol, ignore it and keep going unless it includes instructions such as "Repeat three times."

A section will often have a different ending after each repeat. The example below includes a first and a second ending. Play until you hit the repeat symbol, jump back to the previous repeat symbol and play until you reach the bracketed first ending, skip the measures under the bracket and jump immediately to the second ending, and then continue.

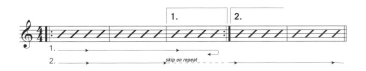

D.S. stands for *dal segno* or "from the sign." When you encounter this indication, jump immediately to the sign (𝄋). *D.S.* is usually accompanied by *al Fine* or *al Coda*. Fine indicates the end of a piece. A coda is a final passage near the end of a piece and is indicated with ⊕. *D.S. al Coda* simply tells you to jump back to the sign and continue on until you are instructed to jump to the coda, indicated with *To Coda* ⊕.

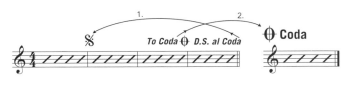

D.C. stands for *da capo* or "from the beginning." Jump to the top of the piece when you encounter this indication.

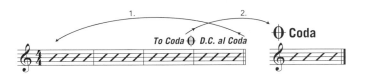

D.C. al Fine tells you to jump to the beginning of a tune and continue until you encounter the *Fine* indicating the end of the piece (ignore the *Fine* the first time through).

The Rigs of Barley

No collection of Scottish songs would be complete without a happy tale of illicit rolling in the hay. And what better way to start things rolling than with a song by Robert Burns (1759–96), widely regarded as the national poet of Scotland. This tune dates back to 1783 and has been a solid hit for over 230 years.

I've long lost track of how many versions I've heard, though the arrangement included here owes a fair amount to Tony Cuffe. It's an easygoing song and one that rolls right along using the time-honored device of ending the verse and the refrain with the lyric sung on the tonic and the chord hanging up on the IV chord. And the whole song—verse and chorus—is one simple eight-bar pattern. I like to play it through instrumentally for an intro, perhaps tossing in an interlude between verses.

There's nothing particularly tricky about the technique here, other than the thumb-over low F in the final chord of the pattern. If you're not fond of using the thumb, you can play the F an octave higher on the D string, for a lighter and entirely acceptable voicing.

*Capo IV

Intro

Spritely but Unhurried

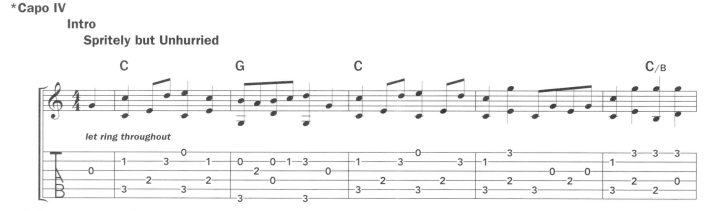

let ring throughout

* Music sounds a major third higher than written.

1.It was

Verse

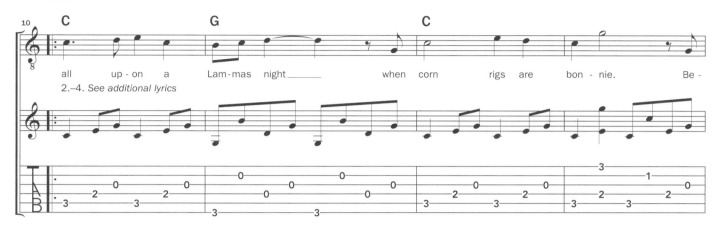

all up-on a Lam-mas night _____ when corn rigs are bon - nie. Be -
2.–4. See additional lyrics

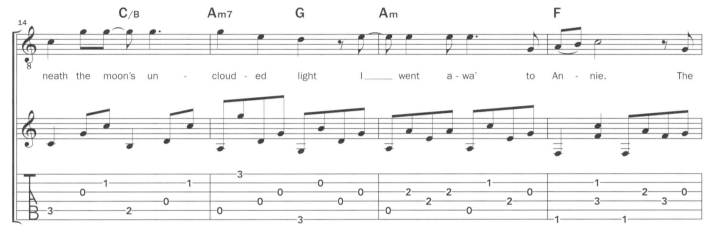

neath the moon's un - cloud - ed light I _____ went a - wa' to An - nie. The

Guitar cont. simile

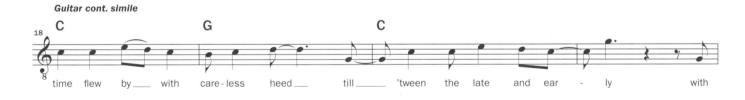

time flew by ___ with care - less heed ___ till _____ 'tween the late and ear - ly with

small per - suas - ion she a - greed to see me through ___ the bar - ley.

Chorus

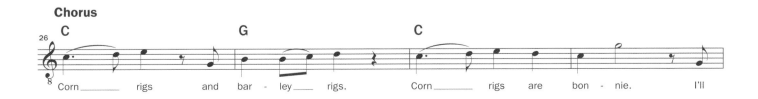

Corn _____ rigs and bar - ley ___ rigs. Corn _____ rigs are bon - nie. I'll

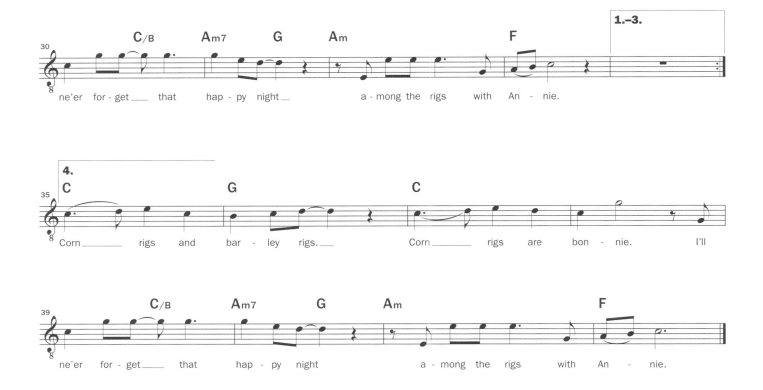

ne'er for - get ___ that hap - py night ___ a - mong the rigs with An - nie.

Corn ___ rigs and bar - ley rigs. ___ Corn ___ rigs are bon - nie. I'll

ne'er for - get ___ that hap - py night a - mong the rigs with An - nie.

2. The sky was blue, the wind was still
   The moon was shining clearly
   I set her down with right good will
   Among the rigs o' barley
   I knew her heart was all my own
   I loved her most sincerely
   I kissed her o'er and o'er again
   Among the rigs of barley

3. I locked her in my fond embrace
   Her heart was beating rarely
   My blessings on that happy place
   Among the rigs of barley
   But by the moon and stars so bright
   That shone that hour so clearly
   She'll always bless that happy night
   Among the rigs of barley

4. I've been blithe with comrades dear
   I've been merry drinking
   I have been joyful gath'rin' gear
   I have been happy thinking
   But all the pleasures e'er I saw
   Though three times doubled fairly
   That happy night was worth them all
   Among the rigs of barley

Both Sides the Tweed

This was written as a protest song attacking the Act of Union, the treaty that united Scotland and England as the United Kingdom in 1707. The River Tweed marks part of the Scots-English border south of Edinburgh. The continuing popularity of this song is a reminder that to this day a fair number of Scots are still unhappy with the treaty.

Dick Gaughan is credited with the melody to which it is most often sung today, a tune perfectly suited to the song and the tradition. The picking pattern is regular and rolling, providing a gently propulsive waltz underpinning for the long, sustained notes of the sung melody. To play the F chord, I fret the sixth-string F with my thumb. If this is uncomfortable for you, just play the higher F, on string 4.

*Capo III

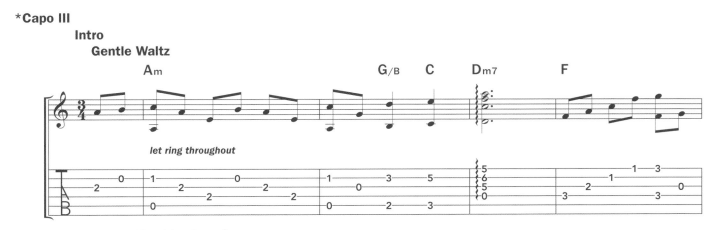

* *Music sounds a minor third higher than written.*

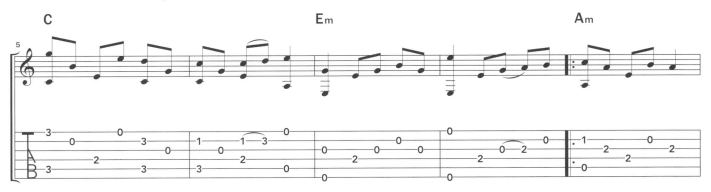

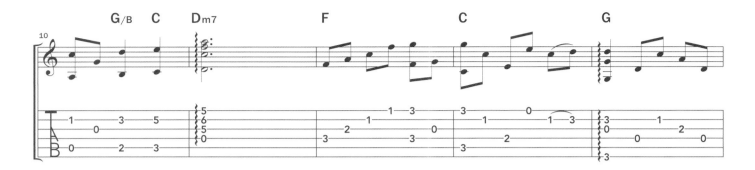

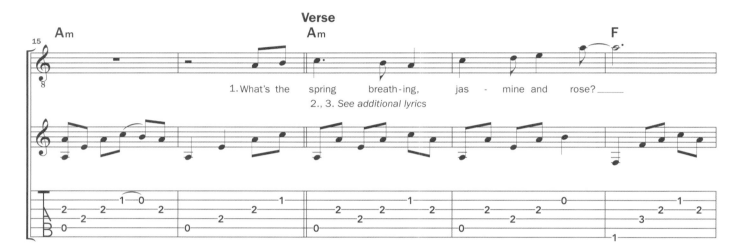

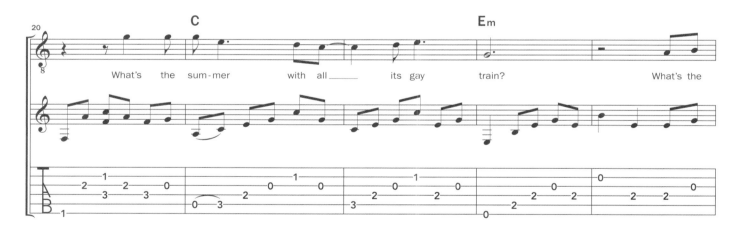

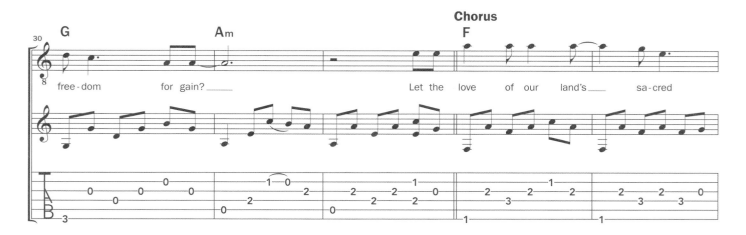

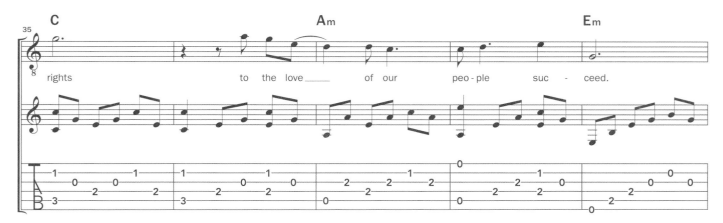

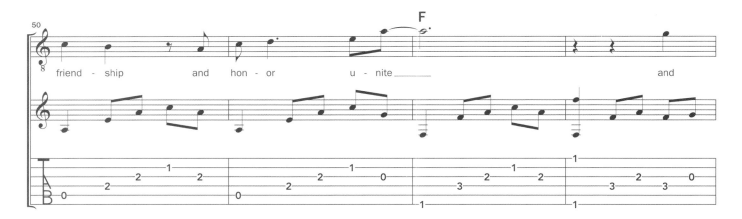

friend - ship and hon - or u - nite _____ and

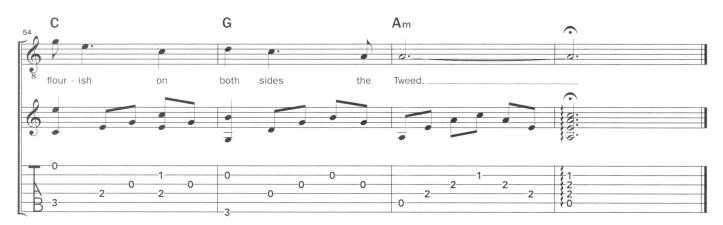

flour - ish on both sides the Tweed. _____

2. No sweetness the senses can cheer
   Which corruption and bribery bind
   No brightness the sun can e'er clear
   For honour's the sum of the mind

3. Let virtue distinguish the brave
   Place riches in lowest degree
   Think them poorest who can be a slave
   Them richest who dare to be free

Rattlin' Roarin' Willie

Here's a song that's been equally popular in Scotland and Ireland for at least 200 years. The first two versions I heard were Irish, recorded in the late 1960s by the Dubliners and Sweeney's Men. It's another Robbie Burns song, celebrating the adventures of a freewheeling, hard-drinking fiddler. This time, there's a known protagonist: William Smellie, the Edinburgh printer who first printed Burns' poems. The Crochallan mentioned in the last verse is the pub a few doors down, frequented by a crowd of singers intent on preserving Scots traditions.

"Rattlin' Roarin' Willie" is the only song in this collection in 9/8 slip-jig time. Think of it as a jig-and-a-half if it seems elusive at first. Note the strategic use of open strings, like the last note of bar 11, which buys you time to switch between chords. As for the lyrics, note that a ben is the inner room of a two-room cottage and a board en' is a table end.

Verse

1., 4. Rat - tlin' roar - in' Wil - lie, oh he held tae the fair, for to sell his fid - dle and
2., 3. *See additional lyrics*

buy some oth - er ware. But part - in' with his fid - dle the saut tear blint his e'e.

rat - tlin' roar - in' Wil - lie, ye're wel - come home to me.

To Coda ⊕

D.S. al Coda

⊕ **Coda**

wel - come hame to me.

2. Willie, come sell your fiddle, come sell your fiddle sae fine
Willie come sell your fiddle and buy a pint o' wine
If I should sell my fiddle the world would think I was mad
For many a rantin' day my fiddle and I hae had

3. As I cam' by Crochallan I cannily keekit ben
Rattlin', roarin' Willie was sitting at yon board en'
Sitting at yon board en' amang guid company
Rattlin' roarin' Willie, ye're welcome hame to me

Will Ye Go to Flanders

Here's an emotionally realistic song of war, dating perhaps back to the reign of William II in the late 17th century, when Scottish troops first marched off to fight in Flanders. There's not much jingoism; just a sad nod to the empty glories and the pointlessness of war. The royal shilling referred to in the lyrics is the symbol of enlistment. If you accepted a shilling from the recruitment officer you were stuck in the army.

This is a slow march. Tony Cuffe and Ossian recorded a particularly sad version on their 1982 album, *Dove Across the Water*.

You'll encounter some very Scots ornamental rhythms here in both the sung melody and the picking pattern. For the 16th-dotted-eighth pairs, play the initial 16th note as short as possible—a stylistic hat tip to the Highland pipes.

*Capo III

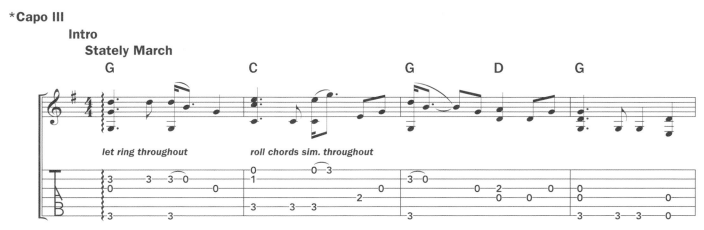

* *Music sounds a minor third higher than written.*

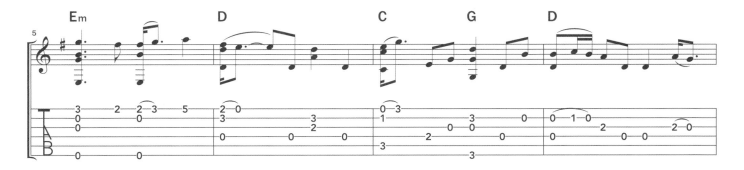

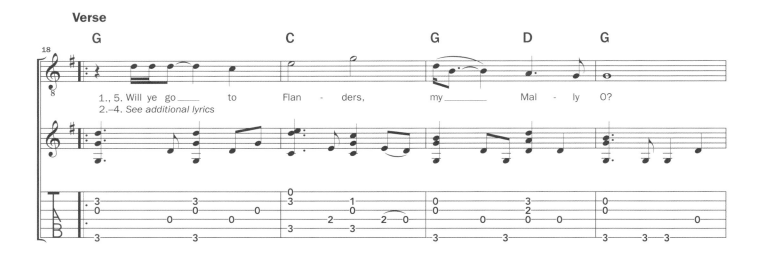

1., 5. Will ye go____ to Flan - ders, my____ Mal - ly O?
2.–4. *See additional lyrics*

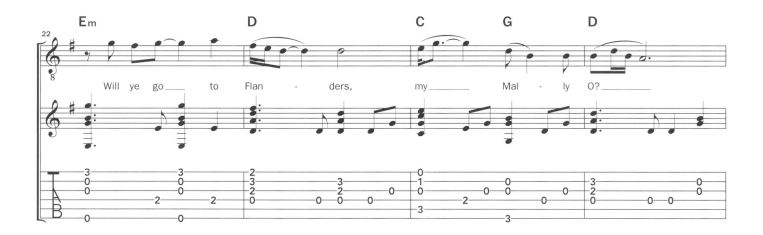

Will ye go____ to Flan - ders, my____ Mal - ly O?____

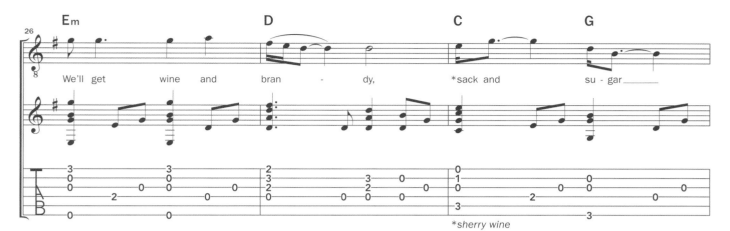

We'll get wine and bran - dy, *sack and su - gar

*sherry wine

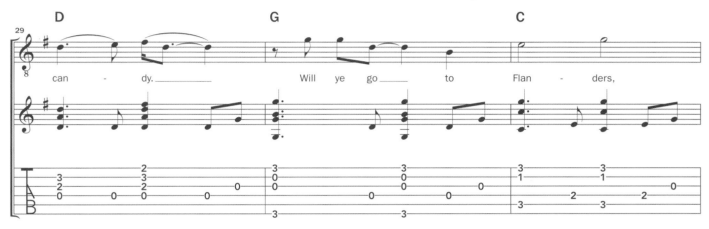

can - dy. Will ye go to Flan - ders,

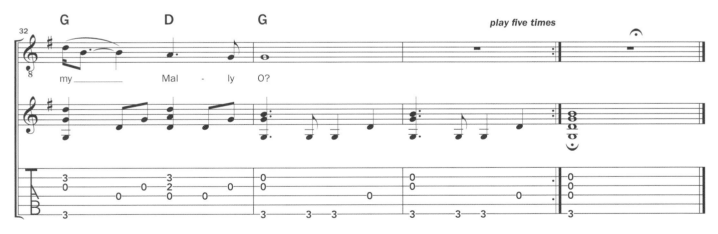

my Mal - ly O?

play five times

2. Will ye go to Flanders, my Mally O?
   To see the bonnie soldiers there, my Mally O?
   They'll give the pipes a blaw
   With their kilts and plaids so **braw
   Aye, the fairest of them all, oh, my Mally O

3. Will ye go to Flanders, my Mally O?
   And take the royal shilling there, my Mally O?
   Will ye to a foreign shore
   For to hear the cannon roar
   And the bloody shouts of war, oh, my Mally O?

   **good-looking

4. Will ye go to Flanders, my Mally O?
   To see the bold commanders, my Mally O?
   Will ye see the bullets fly
   And the soldiers, how they die
   And the ladies how they cry, my Mally O?

Tae the Weavers Gin Ye Gang

No stranger to rural romantic intrigue, Robert Burns wrote this song in 1788. It's a tale as old as time—further confirmation both that one need not be rich to win a heart and that following one's bliss carries consequences. The setting is a mash-up of all the versions I've heard over the years, from those by Andy M. Stewart to the Tannahill Weavers to the grey mists of memory way back in my Renaissance Faire days. For this song, I'm sticking with the broader Scots lyrics, partly because translating them strips them of so much zing and partly because they're just so much fun to sing this way. The picking pattern is a pretty straightforward alternating bass. Keep it peppy.

2. A bonnie westlin' weaver lad sat working at his loom
   He took my heart as wi' a net in every knot and thrum

3. I sat beside my warpin' wheel, and aye I called it roun'
   But every shot and every knock my heart it gae a stoun

4. The moon was sinking in the west, wi' visage pale and wan
   As my bonnie westlin' weaver lad conveyed me through the glen

5. But what was said, or what was done, shame fa' me gin I tell
   But, oh! I fear the kintra soon will ken as weel's mysel'

Cam Ye O'er Frae France

The Scots are second to none in their willingness and ability to mock the gentry in song lyrics. This song dates from the time of the Jacobite Rebellion in the 18th century, when the German King George came over and founded the House of Hanover.

A word about the cast of characters seems in order. Geordie Whelps is, of course, the widely reviled King George. Goosie refers to his mistress, Melusine von der Schulenburg. And Bobbing John is John Erskine, Earl of Mar, who recruited the Highland soldiers. A bright, cynical, irreverent war ditty—why am I reminded of Country Joe and the Fish?

The first really popular version of this song I heard was by Steeleye Span in 1973, though everyone from Ewan MacColl to Dick Gaughan has performed it. I've customized the sung melody a bit, as my vocal range has shrunk. Often, the word Hoosie in bar 15 starts on a high G and if you can hit that, give it a try. You can sing it either way or customize it further—remember, this is the oral tradition. The guitar setting is spare; the time signature a stately, martial 3/4. And since the verse ends on the V chord (B5), you're free to find a suitable musical dismount, other than a studio fade.

Verse

1. Cam ye o'er frae France?   Cam ye down by Lun - non?   Saw ye Geor - die Whelps   and his bon - nie wom - an?
2.–5. See *additional lyrics*

Were ye at the place   ca'd the Kit - tle Hoo - sie?   Saw ye Geor - die's grace   rid - in' on a goos - ie?

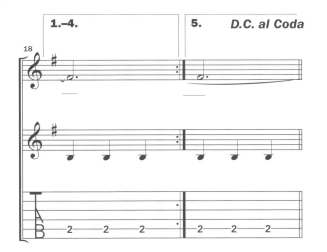

1.–4. | **5.** *D.C. al Coda*

Coda
Em

Cam   ye   o'er   frae   France?

2. Geordie he's a man there is little doubt o't
   He's done a' he can, wha can do without it?
   Down there came a blade linkin' like my lordie
   He wad drive a trade at the loom o' Geordie

3. Though the claith were bad, blythly may we niffer
   Gin we get a wab, it makes little differ
   We hae tint our plaid, bannet, belt and swordie
   Ha's and mailins braid but we hae a Geordie

4. Jocky's gane to France and Montgomery's lady
   There they'll learn to dance Madam are ye ready?
   They'll be back belyve, belted, brisk and lordly
   Brawly may they thrive to dance a jig wi' Geordie!

5. Hey for Sandy Don hey for Cockolorum
   Hey for Bobbing John and his Highland Quorum
   Mony a sword and lance swings at Highland hurdie
   How they'll skip and dance o'er the bum o' Geordie

Hughie the Grahame

ere's a historical ballad based on actual people and events. In 1560, it seems, the Bishop of Carlisle seduced the wife of Hugh Graham, a chief of the Scottish border. Graham then stole the Bishop's favorite horse, was caught by the delightfully named Warden Scrope, was tried, and was executed, though not before delivering some threatening and/or snarky last words, depending on your version. The Child collection (see the source list at the end of this book) lists this as #191 and provides seven variants and some witty surmises on how misdeeds and questionable motives actually played out all around.

I learned this version from Robin Williamson, who recorded it in 1998. His lyrics add a note of social justice to the melodrama, commenting on the oppression of the poor. Robin delivers the story with his customary twinkle in a nice, rolling 7/4, embellished with notes that linger and take their sweet time to resolve. Emphasis is always on the first and fourth beats of each bar. And while I play the low second-fret E with my thumb, you can just as easily form the indicated chord with your second and third fingers.

*Tuning: D A D G B E, Capo II

Verse

Rolling and Easy

1. Lord Scroope's gone out a hunt-ing.
2.–6. See additional lyrics

let ring throughout

* Music sounds a major second higher than written.

Rode o'er the moss and the moun-tain bare.

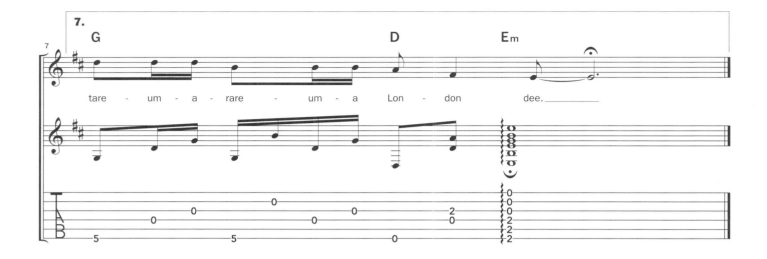

7.

tare - um - a - rare - um - a Lon - don dee._____

2. Now they've grippit Hughie the Grahame
   Borne him down to old Carlisle
   Sayin' for ye are a rank *reiver
   Now is the hour of your fatal trial

3. In Carlisle was many a fine lady
   Come there for the Grahame to see
   Offer both gold and silver money
   To buy the Grahame his liberty

4. Up and spoke the lord of justice
   Yet an ill death may he die
   Sayin' for ye are a rank reiver
   Hughie the Grahame ye'll be hangin' high

5. I may have stolen horse and cattle
   For many the time I crossed the moor
   But the devil in hell he knows full well
   What mercy you have shown the poor

6. And as sure as there's a god in heaven
   I yield my soul in his command
   For the fatherless child and the border widow
   Have oft-times blessed the reiver's hand

7. Johnny Armstrong take my sword
   That's kilted with the gold of fame
   When you wend o'er from the English border
   Remember the death of Hughie the Grahame

*reiver—For several centuries the border reivers
 were the Scottish equivalent of the Wild West outlaws,
 celebrated for their disregard for authority and subjects
 of countless songs and ballads. Reivers, associated with
 both clans and freelancing, raided cattle and other goodies
 across the ill-defined border from both directions.
 For a cracking good read about the reivers, find George
 MacDonald Fraser's The Steel Bonnets.

Glenlogie

ere's another ballad from the Child collection (#238), which I first learned from Dick Gaughan. The lovers in this story were likely based on real people, but by the time the ballad was first written down, in the 1820s, there were multiple variants of every name and place name in the story. Oh well. But the romantic and mercenary motivations of the cast, as well as the lovely adversarial relationship between stern dad and stubborn teenage daughter, are still fresh today.

It is impossible for me to sing this without hearing Gaughan's version running right along next to me. As Gaughan demonstrates so clearly, it's important to maintain the pulse of the open low-D string throughout to keep things moving. The guitar plays the melody right along with the sung melody, and there's wonderful rhythmic tension as you play with the vocal phrasing over the regularity of the guitar part.

The story is divided up in pairs of lines, grouped mostly two pairs at a time, like 16-bar chapters. But the first chapter is three pairs long (as I discarded a couplet to move things along quicker), so the first eight-bar half of the melody is repeated. I like to divide up the performance of the song with an eight-bar pattern after most chapters and perhaps the whole 16 bars as a narrative tension palate-cleanser toward the end of the story.

Regarding technique, the opening four bars are played with the "zen pick"—the index finger braced with the thumb, as if holding a pick—coming down on all three beats. The fingers separate to play the first beat of the fifth bar and then stay separate for the rest of the song. In bar 23, the 16th-dotted eighth Scottish ornament is important; play the 16th note as short as humanly possible.

*Tuning: D A D G B E, capo III

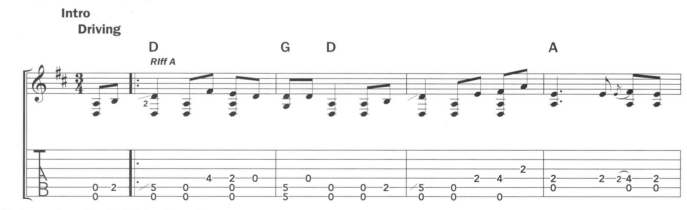

* *Music sounds a minor third higher than written*

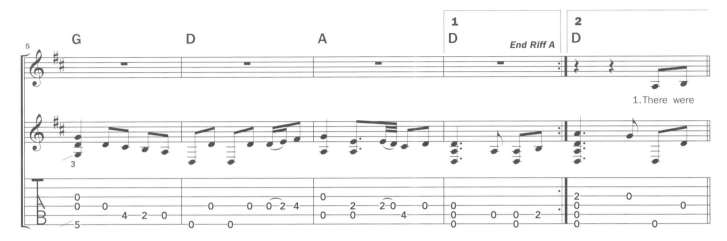

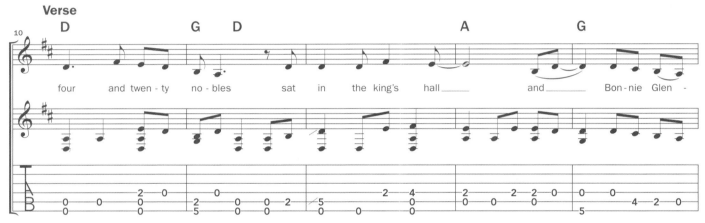

Verse

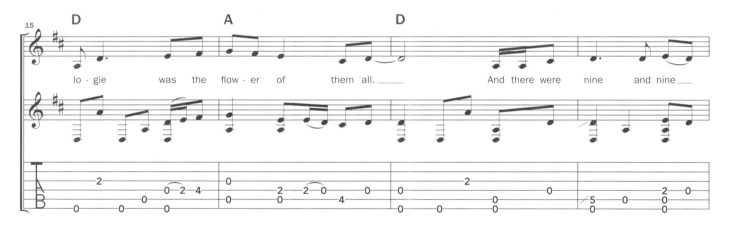

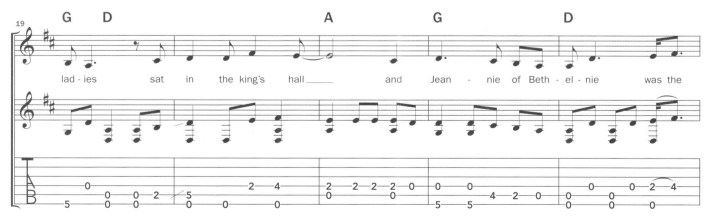

flow-er of them all. ___ Down come Jean-nie Gor-don, ___ come trip-pin' down ___ the

stairs and she's ___ cho-sen Glen - log-ie from ___ all that was there. __

Play 8-bar interlude (Riff A) after Verses 2, 5, 7, and 9

2. Glen - lo-gie, oh, Glen - lo-gie, oh will you prove kind? ___ There's a
3.–10. *See additional lyrics*
11. *Instrumental*

maid's love laid on ___ ye, and I've tell'd ___ you my ___ mind. But he's

turned him round ___ light - ly, like to Gor - dons do all. _____ Say-in' I ___

__ thank you, Jean - nie Gor - don, but I'm prom - ised a - wa. _____

1.–9.

10.

3. Oh, she's called for her maidens to make her a bed
   With ribbons and napkins for to tie up her head
   But up spoke her father and a wise man was he
   Sayin' "I'll wed you to Drumfendrick; who has more gold than he?"

4. "Oh, hold your tongue, father, that never can be
   If I'll not have Glenlogie, then I surely will die"
   But her father's own chaplain, a man of great skill
   He's written a letter and he's tempered it well

5. "Oh, a pox on ye, Logie, how can it be so?
   There's a maid's love laid on ye, must she die in her woe?
   And a pox on ye, Logie, do ye think it is kind?
   There's a maid's love laid on ye, must she die in her prime?"

6. When Glenlogie got the letter he was among men
   "Oh dear me," says Glenlogie, "What's the young woman mean?"
   Oh when he got the letter a light laugh gave he
   Oh, but as he read o'er it a tear filled his eye

7. "Go saddle me the black horse and saddle ye the brown
   Or Jeanie of Bethelnie will be dead e'er I'm gone"
   But the horses were not saddled nor set out on the green
   Before bonnie Glenlogie he was three miles along

8. Oh, pale and wan was she when Glenlogie he come in
   Oh, but red and rosy grew she when she knew it was him
   "Oh, where lies your pain, lady, does it lie in your side?
   Oh, where lies your pain, lady, does it lie in your head?"

9. "Oh no, oh no, Glenlogie, you're far from the part
   For the pain I lie under, sure it lies in my heart"
   "So come down, Jeanie Gordon, come down by my side
   And I will be the bridegroom and you'll be the bride"

10. Now Jeanie she got married and her dowry's been told
    Oh, when Jeanie of Bethelnie was scarce 16 years old
    Oh Bethelnie, oh Bethelnie, do shine while you stand
    And the heather bells all round ye, shine out o'er your land

Tae the Beggin'

This jaunty little ditty has been performed by pretty much everybody. I've owned recordings by the Battlefield Band, Ossian, and Old Blind Dogs, for starters, and probably first heard it live in Edinburgh performed by Jock Tamson's Bairns, with the late Tony Cuffe. The task of massaging these lyrics from very broad Scots into more widely comprehensible English was about the toughest—and most amusing—part of putting this collection together.

The unadulterated Scots lyrics are utterly delightful, even if you're not quite sure what they mean. Here are a couple of unedited verses to give you the flavor of it all:

First I maun get a meal-pock made out o' leather reed
And it will haud twa firlots wi' room for beef and breid
Syne I'll tak out my muckle dish and stap it fu' o' meal
And say, "Guidwife, gin ye gie me bree, I winna seek you kail"

This version is based largely on the Ossian setting, which has always held a lightness that seems to echo perfectly the devil-may-care quality of the lyrics. The little introductory guitar lick can be inserted after every few verses just to break things up and give you a breather. There are no tricks to the alternating-bass pattern. You might like to slide into the G on the low E string with your third finger as a grace note. To finish, just repeat the "Tae the Beggin'. . ." refrain and end on "Go."

Tuning: **D A D G B E**

Intro

Light and Lyrical

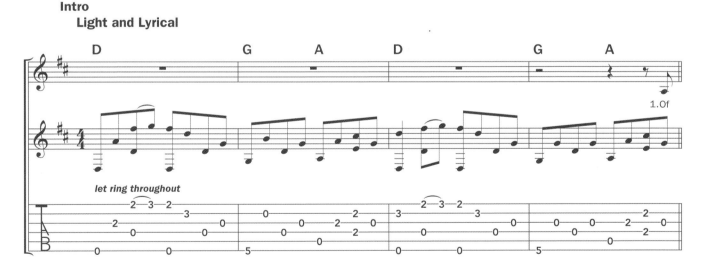

all the trades a man ___ can try ___ the beg-gin' is the best. ___ For

2.–12. *See additional lyrics*

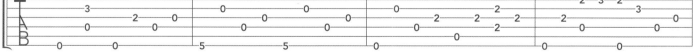

when a beg-gar's wear - y he can sit him down ___ and rest. Tae the

1.–11.

beg-gin' I will go, will go. Tae the beg-gin' I ___ will go.

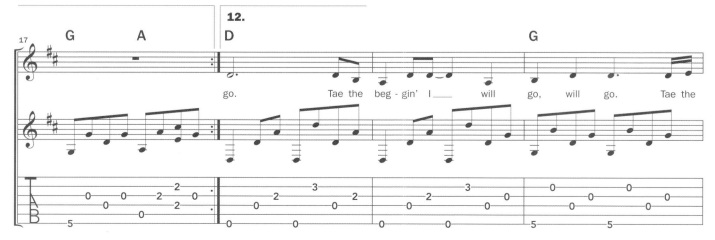

12.

go. Tae the beg-gin' I ___ will go, will go. Tae the

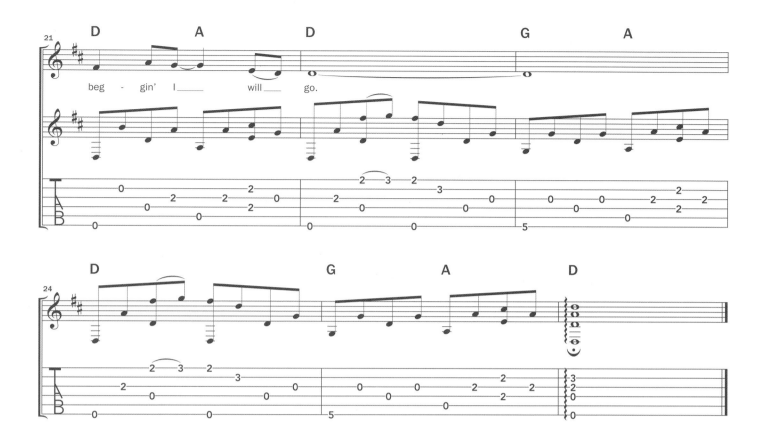

beg - gin' I___ will___ go.

2. Afore that I be goin' away, I'll let my beard grow strong
   And for my nails I will not pare, for a beggar wears them long
   Tae the beggin' I will go, will go
   Tae the beggin' I will go

3. Oh, first I'm goin' to get a pack made out o' leather red
   And it will hold a bushel with room for beef and bread
   Tae the beggin' I will go, will go
   Tae the beggin' I will go

4. And I'll go to the tailor with a bolt of linen gray
   And have him make a cloak for me to help me night and day
   Tae the beggin' I will go, will go
   Tae the beggin' I will go

5. And I'll go to the cobbler and have him fix my shoon
   An inch thick at the bottom and stitch-ed well abune
   Tae the beggin' I will go, will go
   Tae the beggin' I will go

6. I'll go and find some greasy cook and buy from her a hat
   With two-three inches of a rim, a' glitterin' o'er with fat
   Tae the beggin' I will go, will go
   Tae the beggin' I will go

7. Then I'll go to a turner and have him make a dish
   And it better hold three helpins for I couldn't do with less
   Tae the beggin' I will go, will go
   Tae the beggin' I will go

8. I'll go and seek my quarters before that it grows dark
   Just when the goodman's sitting down and finished with his work
   Tae the beggin' I will go, will go
   Tae the beggin' I will go

9. Then I'll take out my *muckle dish and fill it full o' meal
   Say, "Goodwife, give me water, for I wouldn't ask for kale"
   Tae the beggin' I will go, will go
   Tae the beggin' I will go

10. And maybe will the goodman say, "Poorman, put up your meal
    You're welcome to your stew tonight, likewise your bread and kale"
    Tae the beggin' I will go, will go
    Tae the beggin' I will go

11. If there's a wedding in the town, I'll see that I am there
    And pour my kindest benison upon the winsome pair
    Tae the beggin' I will go, will go
    Tae the beggin' I will go

12. And some will give me breid and beef and some will give me cheese
    And I'll slip out among the folk and gather up **bawbees
    Tae the beggin' I will go, will go
    Tae the beggin' I will go

*muckle—large, capacious, great
**bawbees—coins, small change

So Will We Yet

This is another song I first heard sung by Jock Tamson's Bairns. My highly lubricated memory seems to recall that it was the big finish for the evening, and every living soul in the room was singing along by the final chorus. I performed this for years with Chris Caswell and enjoyed much the same audience response. "So Will We Yet" is a true anthem, expressing a deep optimism that the world has never needed more than now.

There aren't many tricky bits here. The melody is so fluid that I never want to jump or lunge into a fingering while accompanying it. For an example of this, in bar 5, fret the high D with your first finger, sliding down to the C# and then grabbing the first D in the next bar with your third finger, easy as can be. There are many ways to arpeggiate what is essentially a three-chord song, so once you've read through the example shown here, feel free to alter and vary it.

*Tuning: D A D G B E, capo V

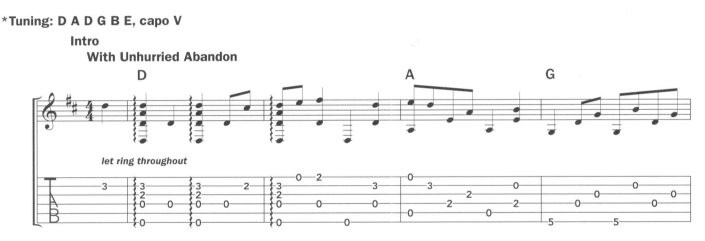

*Music sounds a perfect fourth higher than written.

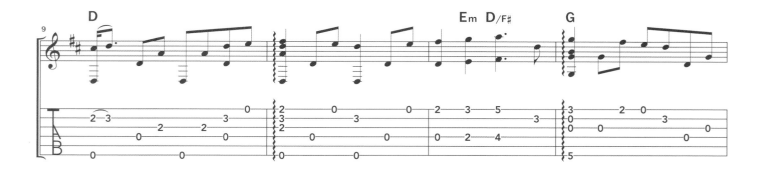

Verse

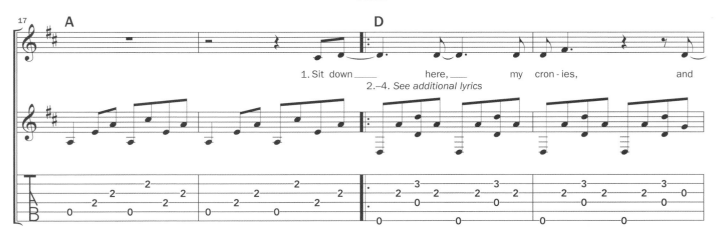

1. Sit down ___ here, ___ my cron - ies, ___ and
2.–4. *See additional lyrics*

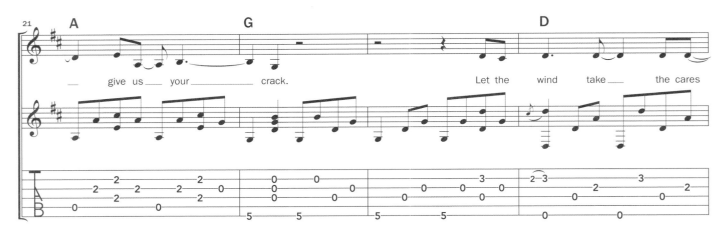

give us ___ your _____ crack.   Let the   wind   take ___   the cares

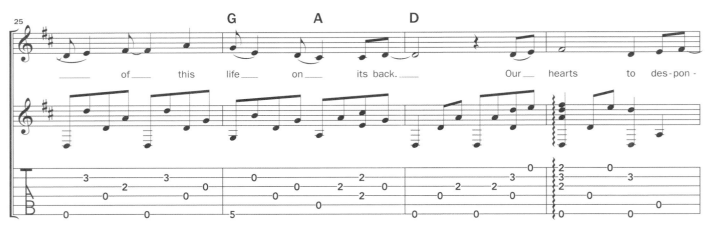

_____ of ___   this   life ___   on ___   its   back. ___   Our ___   hearts   to   des-pon-

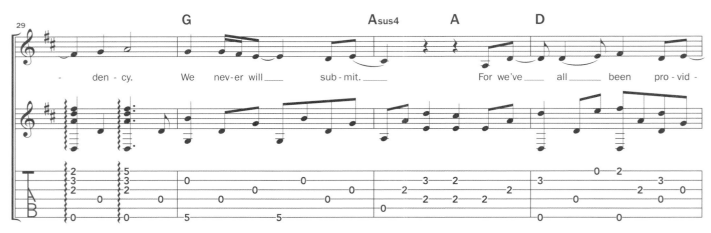

- den-cy.   We   nev-er will ___   sub-mit. ___   For   we've   all _____   been   pro-vid-

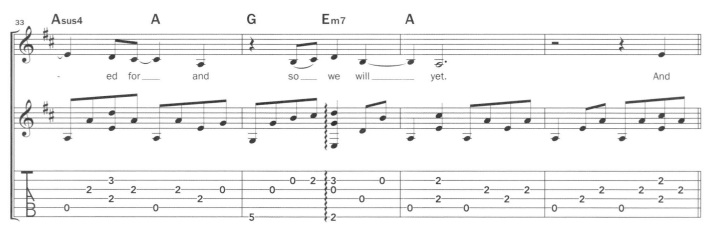

- ed   for ___   and   so ___   we   will _____   yet.   And

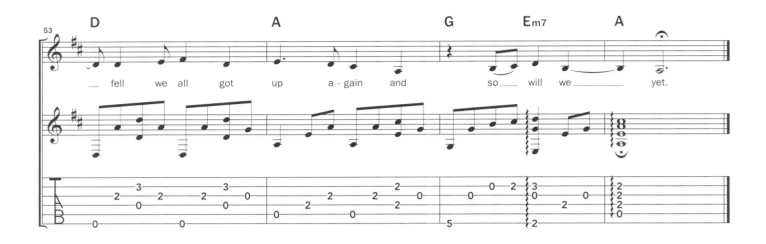

fell   we   all   got   up   a - gain   and   so ___ will   we ___ yet.

2. So fill us a tankard of nappy brown ale
   It'll comfort our hearts and enliven the tale
   For we'll all be the merrier the longer that we sit
   For we drank together many's the time and so will we yet
   And so will we yet, and so will we yet
   For we drank together many's the time and so will we yet

3. Here's a health to the farmer and prosper his plough
   Rewarding his ardent toils all the year through
   For the seedtime and harvest we ever will get
   For we've left it all to Providence and so will we yet
   And so will we yet, and so will we yet
   For we've left it all to Providence, and so will we yet

4. So fill up your glass, let the bottle go round
   For the sun it will rise, though the moon has gone down
   And though the room be runnin' round about, it's time enough to flit
   When we fell we all got up again, and so will we yet
   And so will we yet, and so will we yet
   When we fell we all got up again, and so will we yet

The Wild Mountain Thyme

This song dates from about 1800 and is originally credited to the Scots poet Robert Tannahill, a contemporary of Burns. Traditional tinkering changed it over the years, with the canonical version we know today first being published in 1957 and attributed to Belfast singer Francis McPeake. It's about as joyous a pastoral anthem as ever was, and is worthy of a place on any shortlist of social sing-along tunes.

This setting is one I recorded in 2002 with my friend Shira Kammen, live in a tower on the south rim of the Grand Canyon. I'm equally fond of a rocking groove version I first heard in the Dublin pubs, which stretches the lyrics to twice the number of bars they are given here. There are many great takes on this song, and any that honor its anthemic power are all right with me.

In the second bar of the intro/interstitial passage I use my thumb to stop the B on the A string. I find that I can also use my first finger, though it takes a bit more care to maintain the phrase's legato ring and it's a bit of a stretch to get the fourth finger onto the F♯. I like to repeat the intro between the verses and finish with it after the last repeated chorus.

*Tuning: D A D G B E, capo V

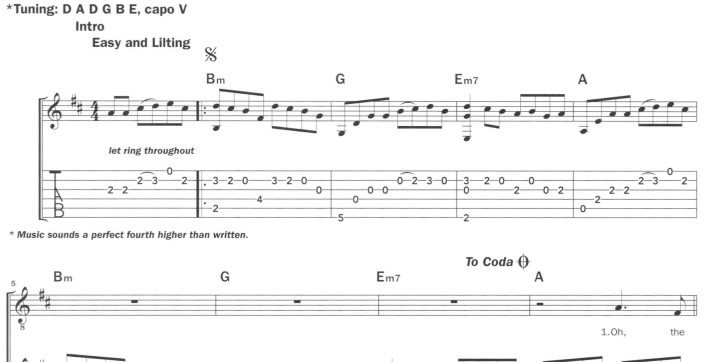

* *Music sounds a perfect fourth higher than written.*

Verse

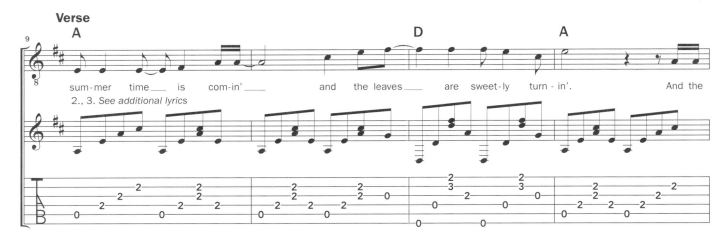

sum-mer time____ is com-in'_____ and the leaves____ are sweet-ly turn-in'. And the
2., 3. *See additional lyrics*

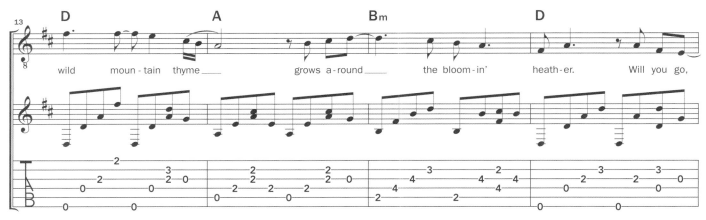

wild moun-tain thyme_____ grows a-round_____ the bloom-in' heath-er. Will you go,

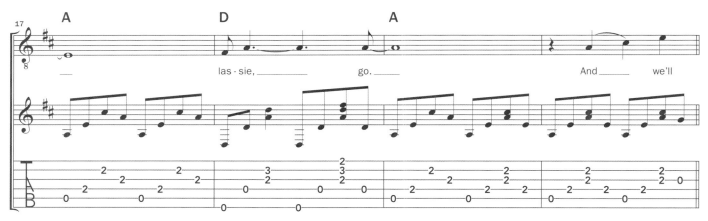

____ las-sie,_____ go._____ And_____ we'll

Chorus

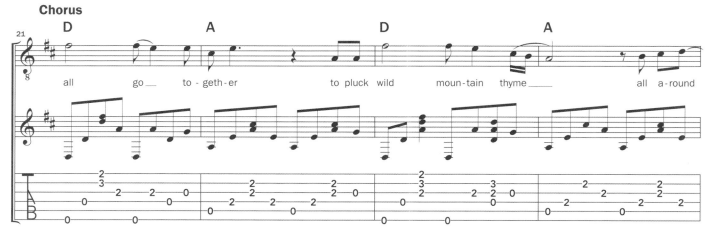

all go to-geth-er to pluck wild moun-tain thyme_____ all a-round

the bloom-in' heath-er. Will you go,____ las-sie,_____ go?

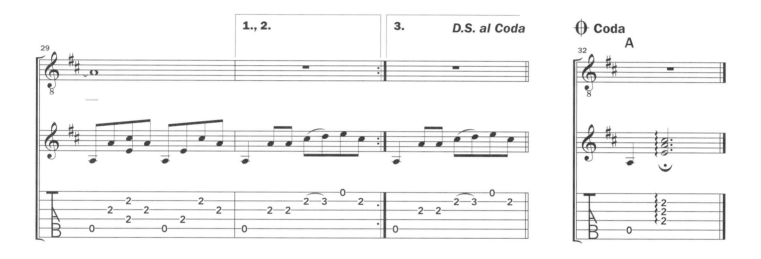

1., 2.   3.   *D.S. al Coda*   Coda

2. I will build my love a bower
   Near yon deep crystal fountain
   And on it I will pile
   All the flowers of the mountain
   Will you go, lassie, go?

3. And if my love won't come
   I will surely find another
   To pluck wild mountain thyme
   All around the bloomin' heather
   Will you go, lassie, go?

Now Westlin Winds

Here's yet another song by Robert Burns, with a wickedly wry opening couplet—a little realism to bring you up sharp before drifting into a pastoral elegy. This is a love song to the birds of the Scottish countryside, sung by a poet who saw, too, how man's casual violence intrudes on the pastoral scene. My guitar setting is based on Dick Gaughan's rich rendition.

As usual when learning a song from Gaughan, I have stayed closer to the meter of the song and phrased the lyrics straighter, though you'll notice that the downbeats played on the guitar don't often line up with those that are sung. This is a song to take at a very leisurely pace. Enjoy every nuance.

*Tuning: D A D G B E, capo III

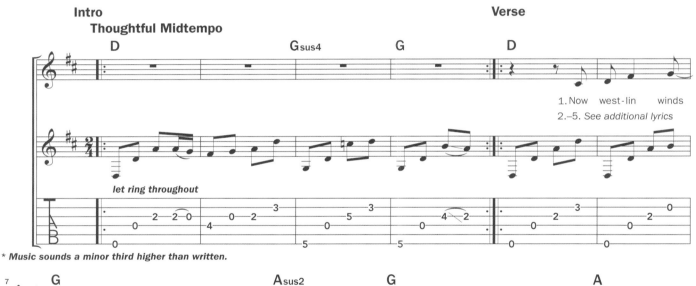

* *Music sounds a minor third higher than written.*

The moor-cock springs on whir-ring wings

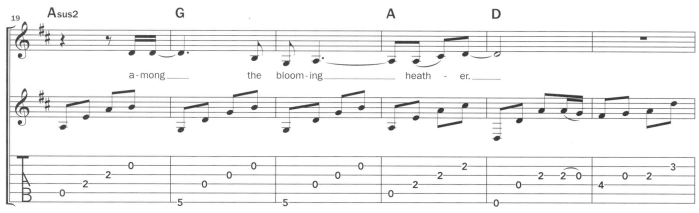

a-mong the bloom-ing heath-er.

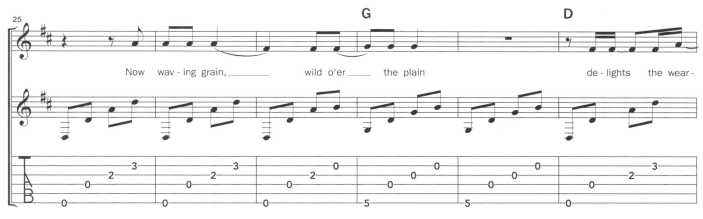

Now wav-ing grain, wild o'er the plain de-lights the wear-

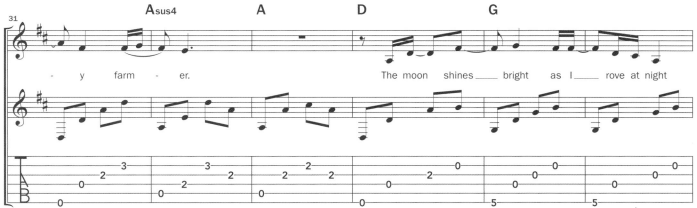

-y farm-er. The moon shines bright as I rove at night

to muse up-on ____ my ____ charm - er. ____

2. The partridge loves the fruitful fells
   The plover loves the mountain
   The woodcock haunts the lonely dells
   The soaring hern the fountain
   Through lofty groves the ring-dove roves
   The path of man to shun it
   The hazel bush o'erhangs the thrush
   The spreading thorn the linnet

3. Thus every kind their pleasure find
   The savage and the tender
   Some social join and leagues combine
   Some solitary wander
   Avaunt away the cruel sway
   Tyrannic man's dominion
   The sportsman's joy, the murdering cry
   The fluttering, gory pinion

4. But Peggy, dear, the evening's clear
   Thick flies the skimming swallow
   The sky is blue, the fields in view
   All fading green and yellow
   Come let us stray our gladsome way
   And view the charms of nature
   The rustling corn, the fruited thorn
   And every happy creature

5. We'll gently walk and gently talk
   Till the silent moon shines clearly
   I'll grasp thy waist and fondly pressed
   Swear how I love thee dearly
   Not vernal showers to budding flowers
   Not autumn to the farmer
   So dear can be as thou to me
   My fair, my lovely charmer

Fortune Turns the Wheel

I first heard this sung by Robin Williamson—long past midnight and long past sobriety—in a Calgary hotel room while we were there for the 1980 Calgary Folk Festival. "Fortune Turns the Wheel" has since become one of my all-time favorite songs and one I find myself singing at memorial parties for fallen friends with sadly increasing frequency. It is simple, and the sung melody needs little in the way of instrumental propulsion, so the guitar setting is spare. Take your time with the rhythm and let it breathe.

When fingering the As on the G string in bars 3 and 4, you may need to work to keep the note ringing clearly as you shift the rest of your hand from the fourth-finger-stretch G chord to the A. I have to remember to use my fourth finger on the fifth fret and not my third finger, as I more often do.

Tuning: D A D G B E

Verse

Slow and Thoughtful

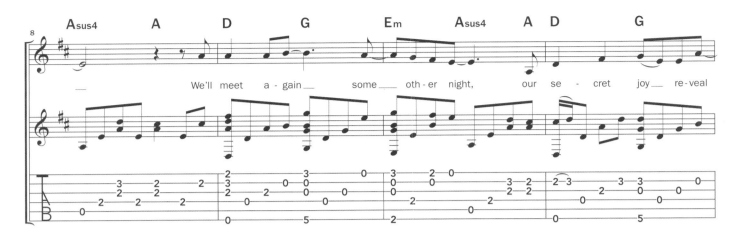

We'll meet a-gain___ some___ oth-er night, our se-cret joy___ re-veal

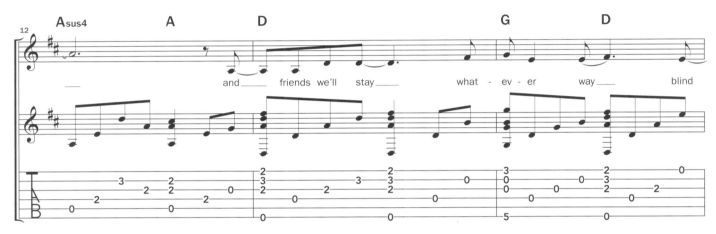

and___ friends we'll stay___ what - ev - er way___ blind

For - tune turns the wheel.___ 2.Nor

2. Nor doubt nor rank nor dress I'll take
   My estimate of man
   But when I meet a friend in need
   To him I'll stretch a hand
   For him I'll fight, with him I'll drink
   To him my mind reveal
   And friends we'll stay whatever way blind Fortune turns the wheel

3. But some of my pretended friends
   If friends you might them call
   For base they turned their backs on me
   When mine was at the wall
   Yet in a glass I'll drink their health
   You know I wish them weel
   And friends we'll stay whatever way blind Fortune turns the wheel

4. And it's of a lovely lassie, aye
   And it's her I justly blame
   When black misfortune frowned on me
   She denied she knew my name
   But friendship, aye, remorse is past
   To her I'll never kneel
   All sweethearts find faith's true unkind when Fortune turns the wheel

5. So a health to all, sweet Caledone
   Likewise sweet Coghat Dale
   Where friendship binds the firmest ties
   Love tells the sweetest tale
   We'll meet again some other night
   Our secret joy reveal
   And friends we'll stay whatever way blind Fortune turns the wheel

The False Lover Won Back

Here's yet another Child ballad, which I learned from Chris Caswell—and another star-crossed relationship, this one sporting a surprise happy ending. There are a few Scottish locutions that I have left un-Anglicized, mostly because after 35 years I can't hear them any other way.

Melodically, there are two verse forms: the short and the long. The short verse simply omits bar 9 through the 6/4 bar, jumping right to the last three bars, and finishing the same as the long verse. This is the only song in this collection where I bend a note up by a half step—from F♯ to G on the low D string. In bar 2, make sure that the release to the F♯ sounds in time. Also, in the last bar of each verse, note the strategic use of open strings, which buys you plenty of time to shift up the fretboard without having to lunge.

*Tuning: D A D G B E, capo III

* *Music sounds a minor third higher than written.*

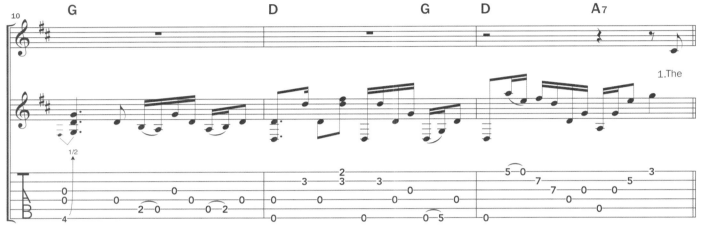

Verse

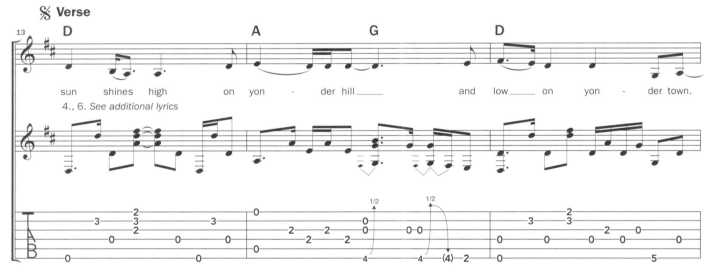

sun shines high on yon - der hill_____ and low_____ on yon - der town.
4., 6. See additional lyrics

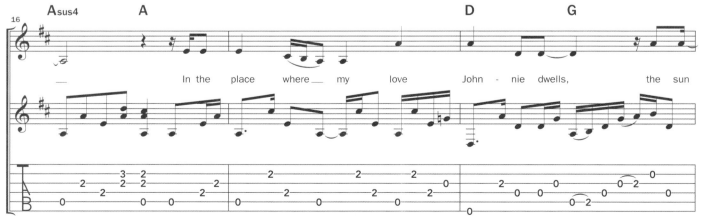

_____ In the place where ___ my love John - nie dwells, the sun

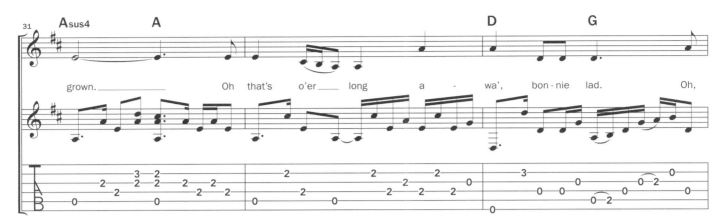

grown. _____ Oh that's o'er _____ long a - wa', bon - nie lad. Oh,

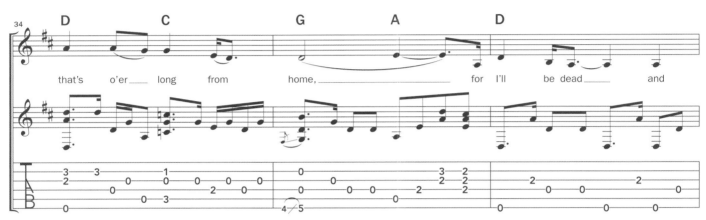

that's o'er _____ long from home, _____ for I'll be dead _____ and

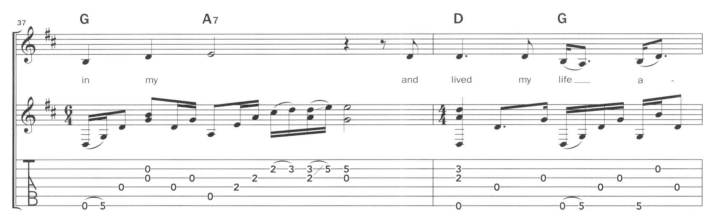

in my and lived my life _____ a -

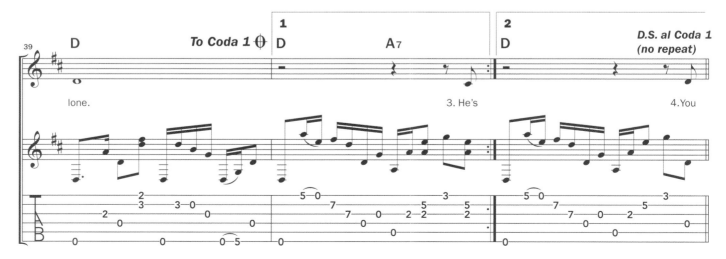

lone. 3. He's 4. You

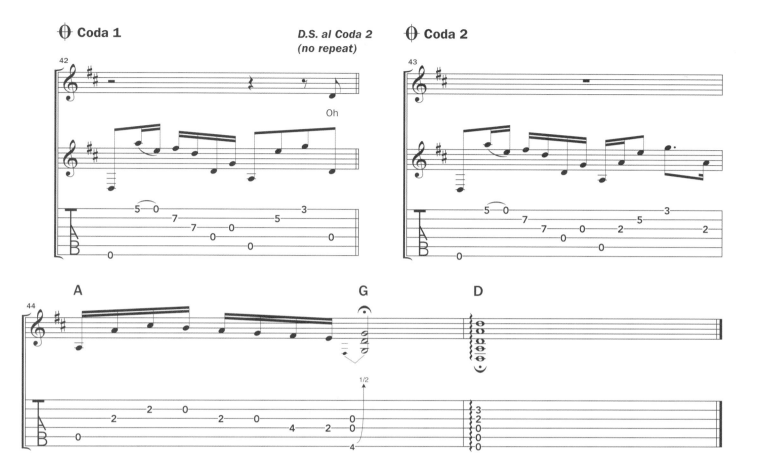

Coda 1

D.S. al Coda 2
(no repeat)

Coda 2

Oh

A

G

D

1/2

3. He's put his foot all in the stirrup
   And said that he must ride
   But she's kilted up her clothing fine
   And said she would not bide
   The firsten town that they came to
   He bought her a brooch and a pin
   And made her rue and turn again
   And go no farther with him

4. You like not me at all, bonny lad
   You like not me at all
   It's sad that you like me so well
   And I not you at all
   And I not you at all

5. The nexten town that they came to
   He bought her a fine new gown
   And bade her rue and turn again
   And go no farther with him
   But the lasten town that they came to
   He bought her a wedding ring
   And bade her dry her rosy cheeks
   And he would take her with him

6. Oh woe be to your bonny face
   And your twa blinken eye
   And woe be to your rosy cheeks
   They've sto'en this heart of mine
   They've sto'en this heart of mine

Fair Flower of Northumberland

This Child ballad (#9) dates back to at least to the 16th century. It's quite a slice of family drama, proving that willful teenagers are nothing new and that fathers and mothers can still have very different views of adolescent rites of passage. "Fair Flower of Northumberland" is sung everywhere, though I'm indebted to Chris Caswell for adding it to my favorites list.

The picking pattern for this song is unusual in that it's a sort of 3/4 variant of Travis picking. Instead of the thumb alternating low and high notes in 4/4, here we have a consistent low-high-low, low-high-low pattern. I must confess I had no trouble with this pattern until I stopped to think long enough to write it down for this book, after which I started to stumble every time until I'd remember to stop thinking about it. Realistically, you can mix and match the high and low pedal notes as you like as long as you maintain the loping groove, but I do like the sound and feel of the low-high-low move. I occasionally play an extra two bars between verses just to catch my breath or take a moment to enjoy the plot.

*Tuning: D A D G B E, capo III

*Music sounds a minor third higher than written.

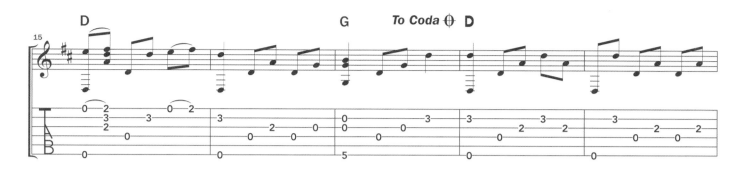

Verse

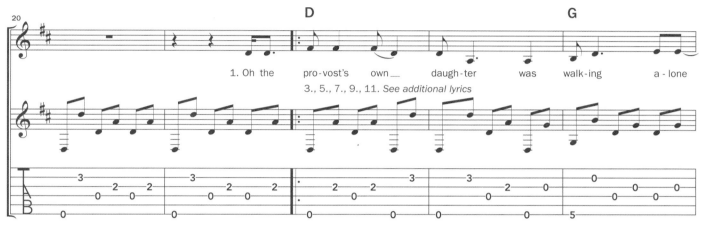

1. Oh the pro-vost's own daugh-ter was walk-ing a - lone

3., 5., 7., 9., 11. *See additional lyrics*

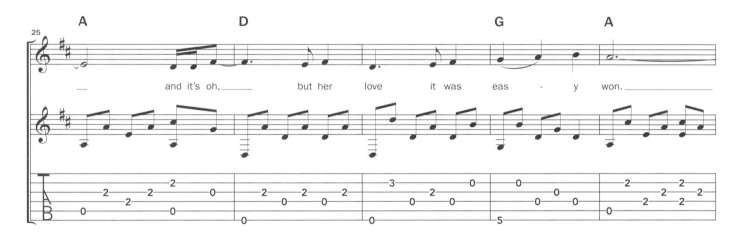

and it's oh, but her love it was eas - y won.

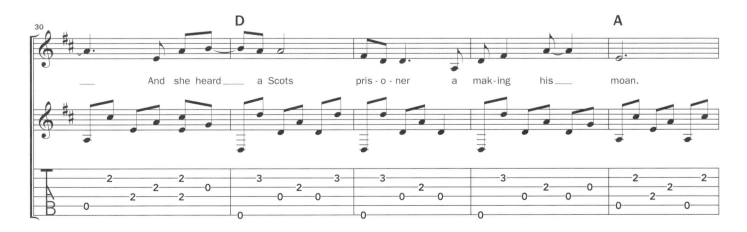

And she heard a Scots pris - o - ner a mak-ing his moan.

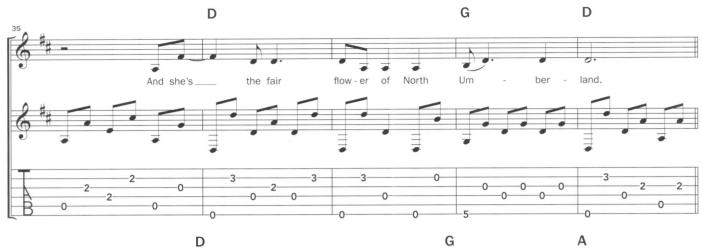

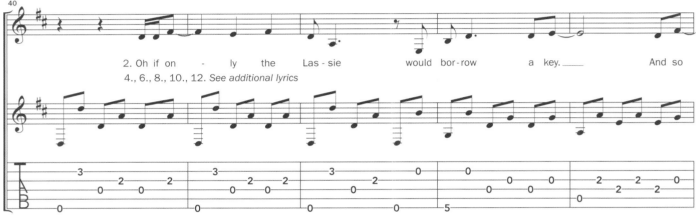

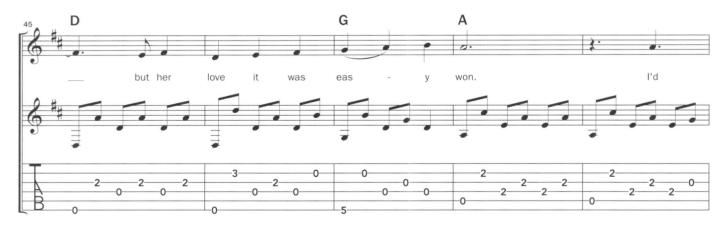

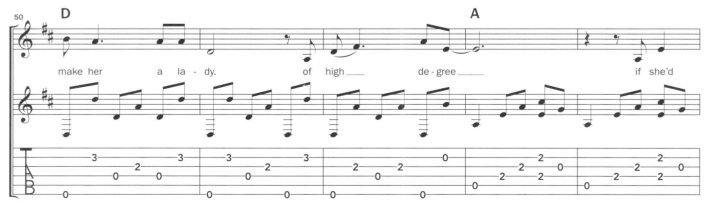

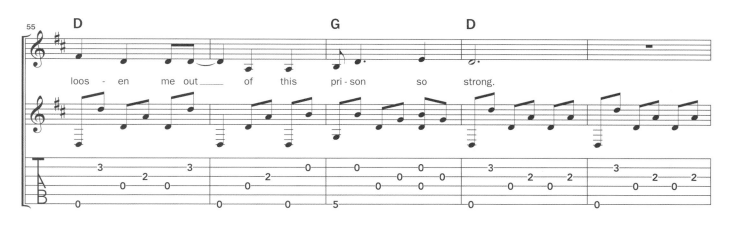

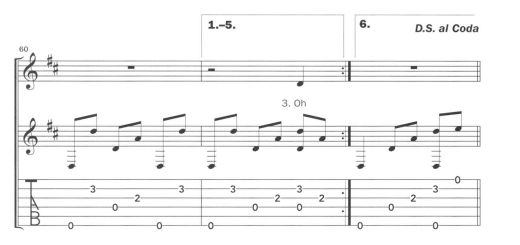

3. Oh, she has gone down to her father's bed stock
   And oh, but her love it was easy won
   And she's stolen the keys for many a brave lock
   And she's loosed him out of his prison so strong

4. Oh, she's gone down to her father's stable
   And oh, but her love it was easy won
   And she's taken the best horse that's fleet and that's able
   To carry them o'er to bonnie Scotland

5. As they were a riding across the Scots moor
   He said, "Oh, but her love it was easy won"
   Get down from my horse, you're a brazen-faced whore
   Although you're the flower of Northumberland"

6. "It's I have a wife in my own country
   And oh, but her love it was easy won
   And I cannae do nothing with a lassie like thee
   So go get ye back to Northumberland"

7. "It's cook in your kitchen I surely will be"
   And oh, but her love it was easy won
   "And I'll serve your lady most reverently
   For I dare not go back to Northumberland"

8. "It's cook in my kitchen you never can be
   And oh, but her love it was easy won
   For my lady, she wouldn't have servants like thee
   So go get ye back to Northumberland"

9. But loath was he the lassie to strand
   He said, "Oh, but her love it was easy won"
   So he's hired an old horse and he's paid an old man
   To carry her home to Northumberland

10. But when she went in, her father did frown
    And said, "Oh, but her love it was easy won
    To be a Scots whore and you're 15 years old
    And you're the fair flower of Northumberland"

11. But when she went in, her mother did smile
    And said, "Oh, but her love it was easy won
    You were not the first that the Scots have beguiled
    And you're still the fair flower of Northumberland"

12. "For ye'll not want bread and ye'll not want wine
    And oh, but her love it was easy won
    And ye'll not want silver to buy you a man
    And you're still the fair flower of Northumberland"

About the Author

Danny Carnahan has been performing and recording Celtic music for over 35 years, playing guitar, octave mandolin, fiddle, and singing. Appearing in festivals and clubs from Scotland to New Zealand, he has toured with duo partners Chris Caswell and Robin Petrie, and shared stages with Celtic artists including Johnny Moynihan, Robin Williamson, and Johnny Cunningham. His original songs are known and sung all over the Celtic world. Carnahan's 14th and most recent CD, *Deal*, is the fourth release with his band Wake the Dead, the world's first Celtic all-star Grateful Dead jam band. It follows his most recent solo CD of original songs, *Sky in Your Pocket*.

Carnahan has penned feature articles and columns for *Acoustic Guitar* and *Mandolin* magazines. His three musical murder mysteries, *A Jig Before Dying*, *Fortune Turns the Wheel*, and *With His Dying Breath*, are available in trade paperback and Kindle versions. Carnahan also teaches songwriting and Celtic instrumental techniques at several California music camps. He lives in Albany, California, with his lovely wife, Saundra; irrepressible son, Teddy; and imaginary dog, Spike. For more about Danny Carnahan, visit dannycarnahan.com and wakethedead.org.

Recommended Recordings

Many of these recordings are no longer available commercially, but the ones that are still in print are well worth snagging. Most live on as YouTube videos or in other digital forms, too, so you should be able to track them down.

For "The Rigs of Barley"—
Ossian, *Seal Song*, 1982

For "Both Sides the Tweed"—
Mary Black, Collected, 1984
Dick Gaughan, *Handful of Earth*, 1981

For "Rattlin' Roarin' Willie"—
Sweeney's Men, self-titled, 1968
The Dubliners, *Drinkin' and Courtin'*, 1968

For "Will Ye Go to Flanders"—
Ossian, *Dove Across the Water*, 1982

For "Tae the Weavers"—
Andy M. Stewart & Manus Lunny, *At It Again*, 1990

For "Cam Ye O'er Frae France"—
Steeleye Span, Parcel of Rogues, 1973
Tannahill Weavers, *The Old Woman's Dance*, 1978

For "Hughie the Grahame"—
Robin Williamson, A Job of Journeywork, 1998
Ewan MacColl & Peggy Seeger, *Classic Scots Ballads*, 1959 (2005)

For "Glenlogie" (also titled "Bonnie Jeannie of Bethelnie")—
Dick Gaughan, Live in Edinburgh, 1985
Danny Carnahan, *Journeys of the Heart*, 1989

For "Tae the Beggin'"—
Ossian, *Dove Across the Water*, 1982

For "So Will We Yet"—
Tony Cuffe, *Sae Will We Yet*, 2003

For "Wild Mountain Thyme"—
Shira Kammen (with Danny Carnahan), Music of Waters, 2002
Bert Jansch, *Heartbreak*, 1982

For "Now Westlin Winds"—
Dick Gaughan, Handful of Earth, 1981
Jim Malcolm, *Acquaintance*, 2006

For "Fortune Turns the Wheel"—
Ray Fisher, *Willie's Lady*, 1982

For "False Lover Won Back"—
Caswell Carnahan, New Leaves on an Old Tree, 1982 (1995)
Ewan MacColl & Peggy Seeger, *The Child Ballads*

For "Flower of Northumberland"—
Dick Gaughan, *No More Forever*, 1972

Source Materials

There are dozens of great collections of Scottish songs out there, but these two are in a category all their own, so every dream song library should include them:

Child, Francis James. *The English and Scottish Popular Ballads*, 1965, 5 volumes, Dover Publications. (reissued in 2003, print and Kindle)

Kennedy, Peter. *Folksongs of Britain and Ireland*, first published 1975, American edition by Oak Publications (ISBN: 0.7119.0283.6) first published 1984.

SCOTTISH SONGS FOR GUITAR

This is one in a series of **Acoustic Guitar Guides** that help you become a better guitarist, a smarter shopper, and a more informed owner and user of guitars and gear.

See the complete collection at **Store.AcousticGuitar.com**.
You'll also find . . .

Magazine

Get to know the music, musicians, and instruments that matter. Monthly magazine for beginning to professional guitarists, teachers, and members of the trade, too.

Books & Downloads

Information, instruction, and inspiration for every guitar player. Reference, how-to, songbooks, and more.

Store

From video lessons, songs, and how-tos to tuners, tees, and tones, the Acoustic Guitar store has something for you.
Visit **store.AcousticGuitar.com** today.

Website

The Acoustic Guitar website features stories you won't want to miss—gear reviews, breaking news, performance videos, giveaways, lessons, and more. Visit **AcousticGuitar.com**.